EXPLORING COUNTRIES
India

by Jim Bartell

BELLWETHER MEDIA • MINNEAPOLIS, MN

Note to Librarians, Teachers, and Parents:

Blastoff! Readers are carefully developed by literacy experts and combine standards-based content with developmentally appropriate text.

Level 1 provides the most support through repetition of high-frequency words, light text, predictable sentence patterns, and strong visual support.

Level 2 offers early readers a bit more challenge through varied simple sentences, increased text load, and less repetition of high-frequency words.

Level 3 advances early-fluent readers toward fluency through increased text and concept load, less reliance on visuals, longer sentences, and more literary language.

Level 4 builds reading stamina by providing more text per page, increased use of punctuation, greater variation in sentence patterns, and increasingly challenging vocabulary.

Level 5 encourages children to move from "learning to read" to "reading to learn" by providing even more text, varied writing styles, and less familiar topics.

Whichever book is right for your reader, Blastoff! Readers are the perfect books to build confidence and encourage a love of reading that will last a lifetime!

This edition first published in 2011 by Bellwether Media, Inc.

No part of this publication may be reproduced in whole or in part without written permission of the publisher. For information regarding permission, write to Bellwether Media, Inc., Attention: Permissions Department, 5357 Penn Avenue South, Minneapolis, MN 55419.

Library of Congress Cataloging-in-Publication Data

Bartell, Jim.
  India / by Jim Bartell.
     p. cm. – (Blastoff! readers: Exploring countries)
  Includes bibliographical references and index.
  Summary: "Developed by literacy experts for students in grades three through seven, this book introduces young readers to the geography and culture of India"–Provided by publisher.
  ISBN 978-1-60014-555-1 (paperback : alk. paper)
  1. India–Juvenile literature. I. Title.
  DS407.B348 2010
  954–dc22   2010009210

Printed in the United States of America, North Mankato, MN.

080110   1170

Contents

China

Pakistan

Nepal

Bhutan

New Delhi

India

Bangladesh

Myanmar

Arabian
Sea

Bay of
Bengal

Palk
Strait

Indian
Ocean

Gulf of
Mannar

Sri Lanka

India is a country in southern Asia. With an area of
1,269,219 square miles (3,287,263 square kilometers), it is
the seventh-largest country in the world. Most of India is a
peninsula that sticks out into the Indian Ocean. The capital
of India is New Delhi.

The Arabian Sea lies to the west of India, and the Bay of Bengal lies to the east. India shares borders with Pakistan, China, Nepal, Bhutan, Myanmar, and Bangladesh. Sri Lanka, an island nation, lies about 19 miles (31 kilometers) off the southern coast of India. The two countries are separated by the **Gulf** of Mannar and the Palk Strait.

India has a wide range of land features, including deserts, plains, jungles, and forests. The Himalayan Mountains tower over northern India. South of the mountains is the lush Ganges Plain, which covers much of northern and central India. In western India, dry winds blow across the hot Thar Desert. The Deccan **Plateau** lies in central and southern India. Tropical jungles can be found in the southern parts of the country. Many wild animals live in the **mangrove forests** to the east.

There are several rivers in India. The Ganges and the Brahmaputra are two major rivers that run through India. Parts of five Indus River **tributaries** also flow through the country.

Jog Falls

mangrove forest

Thar Desert

! fun fact

The word *Himalaya* is a combination of the Sanskrit words *hima*, which means "snow," and *alaya*, which means "home."

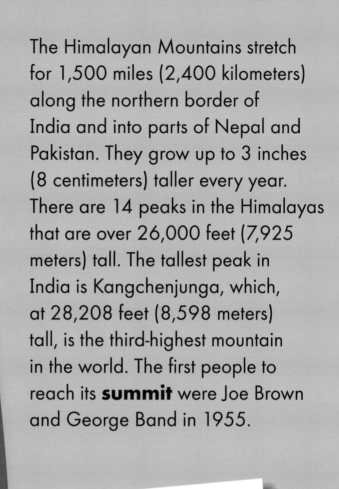

The Himalayan Mountains stretch for 1,500 miles (2,400 kilometers) along the northern border of India and into parts of Nepal and Pakistan. They grow up to 3 inches (8 centimeters) taller every year. There are 14 peaks in the Himalayas that are over 26,000 feet (7,925 meters) tall. The tallest peak in India is Kangchenjunga, which, at 28,208 feet (8,598 meters) tall, is the third-highest mountain in the world. The first people to reach its **summit** were Joe Brown and George Band in 1955.

Kangchenjunga

peacock

fun fact

More than 1,200 kinds of birds live in India, including the peacock, its national bird.

India is home to a variety of animals. Bengal tigers live in the forests, hills, and mountainous regions of India. The rarely seen snow leopard hides in the Himalayas. The jungles of southern India are home to leopards, Asiatic lions, Asian elephants, and the Indian rhinoceros. Crocodiles hunt in many rivers throughout India.

Did you know?
India is the only country in the world that has both lions and tigers in the wild.

Asian elephant

Bengal tiger

lotus

The single-humped camel can be found in the deserts of western India. The red panda, the long-tailed monkey, and the striped hyena also live in India. There are 15,000 flowering plants in India. The lotus, **native** to India, is the national flower of India. It grows in water and has large, flat leaves and beautiful pink flowers.

! fun fact

India has the largest population of Hindus in the world. The estimated number of Hindus in India is approaching one billion!

With almost 1.2 billion people, India is the second most populated country in the world. Families in India are often large. Children live with their parents and grandparents. Sometimes aunts, uncles, and cousins live with them too.

Many languages are spoken in India. Twenty-nine of the languages have over 1,000,000 native speakers each. Hindi is the official language of India. About 4 out of 10 Indians speak Hindi. English is a secondary official language. It is often used for national, political, and business purposes.

Speak Hindi!

English	Hindi	How to say it
hello	namaste	nah-MUH-stay
good-bye	namaste	nah-MUH-stay
yes	haan	hahn
no	nahi	nah-hee
please	kripaya	kri-pah-yah
thank you	dhanyavad	DHAN-yah-vaad
friend	dost	DOH-st

Daily life in India is very different in the city than it is in the country. In cities such as Mumbai, most people live in one-room apartments. People have many neighbors because apartment buildings are large and crowded. Indians use trains, bicycles, and buses to get around town. Many Indians also walk from place to place. They shop in outdoor markets, small stores, and malls.

Where People Live in India

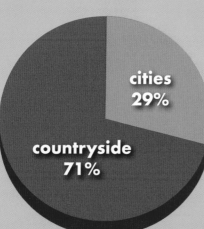

cities
29%

countryside
71%

While city life in India is busy and noisy, life in India's villages is quiet. Many of the villages share common facilities like grazing grounds for animals, water wells, and temples. Most villagers farm small plots of land and grow very little food.

Did you know?

For many Indians, prayer is a part of daily life. Many Indians must pray at certain times of the day to practice their religion.

Did you know?
About 4 out of 10 Indians cannot read or write.

Public school for Indian children is free until the age of 14. After that, parents have to pay for books, **tuition**, and uniforms. Textbooks are expensive and often hard to find. Many children quit school so they can work and help support their families. Children who stay in school study science, math, grammar, and spelling. They may also take classes in art, English, and physical education.

Many classrooms in India have more than 50 students. Only one out of five children graduates from secondary school, where they learn many job skills. University, the next level of education, is expensive and demanding. Only one out of ten Indians attends. University students study subjects like medicine, law, and **information technology**.

Working

fun fact

India is the world's largest tea producer. Tea is its most popular beverage.

Where People Work in India

services 34%

farming 52%

manufacturing 14%

Work is different for Indians who live in cities and those who live in the countryside. Indians who work in cities often work 12-hour days. Many Indians work in shops, malls, restaurants, and hotels. Others work in factories that produce **textiles**, chemicals, and other goods. Miners outside of cities dig up coal, diamonds, and other **natural resources** from the earth.

A little more than half of all Indians are farmers. They rise early in the morning to grow peanuts, rice, cotton, wheat, potatoes, and tea. Some farmers tend to their sheep, goats, and chickens. Many villages have large ponds or lakes where fish are raised. Fishing is also important along India's coasts.

Indians spend their free time doing many activities. The most popular sports in India are **cricket**, field hockey, and soccer. Many Indian children begin playing these sports at a very young age. Indians also enjoy dancing and playing games. One of their favorite board games is chess, which was invented in India more than 1,500 years ago.

Indians spend a lot of time talking with and enjoying the company of neighbors. They also love to go to movies. Every major city has several movie theaters. The Indian movie industry is nicknamed "Bollywood." India makes more movies each year than any other country in the world!

fun fact

Bollywood movies are mostly musicals. They feature songs and dances that tell parts of a story.

fun fact

In India, people often eat with their hands. The right hand will scoop the food up with *roti* or *naan*, both kinds of flatbread.

For many Indians, their **diet** is part of their religion. Hindus do not eat beef, and Muslims do not eat pork. However, there are many dishes that all people living in India enjoy. Curry is a spicy, creamy stew that is popular across India. A common snack, *bhelpuri*, is a mix of puffed rice, chickpeas, onions, tomatoes, and green peppers. **Chutney** is served with main dishes throughout India.

lassi

curry

Lassi is a traditional cold drink made of yogurt or buttermilk with rose or mango flavors. It can also be served plain. Some food is only popular in certain parts of India. In the north, **tandoori ovens** are used to cook vegetables and meat. Seafood is a common item along the coasts, and rice is served with almost every meal in the south.

Festival of Color

Many of India's holidays are religious celebrations. The Hindu religion has the Festival of Lights called *Diwali* in the fall. Homes are decorated with lights, and fireworks explode in the sky. The Hindu spring festival is the Festival of Color, or *Holi*. People throw colored water and powder at each other to celebrate. Muslims observe **Ramadan**. This is a month in which Muslims **fast** from sunrise until sunset to practice modesty and patience.

India has many national holidays. Indians celebrate Republic Day on January 26. It was on this day in 1950 that India's **constitution** became the law of the land. On August 15, Indians celebrate Independence Day. This is the day they gained independence from the **United Kingdom (U.K.)**. A few months later, on October 2, Indians celebrate the birthday of Mohandas Gandhi. He helped India gain independence from the British using **non-violent protest**.

Gandhi

The Taj Mahal

Did you know?

The Taj Mahal was recently named one of the Seven Wonders of the Modern World.

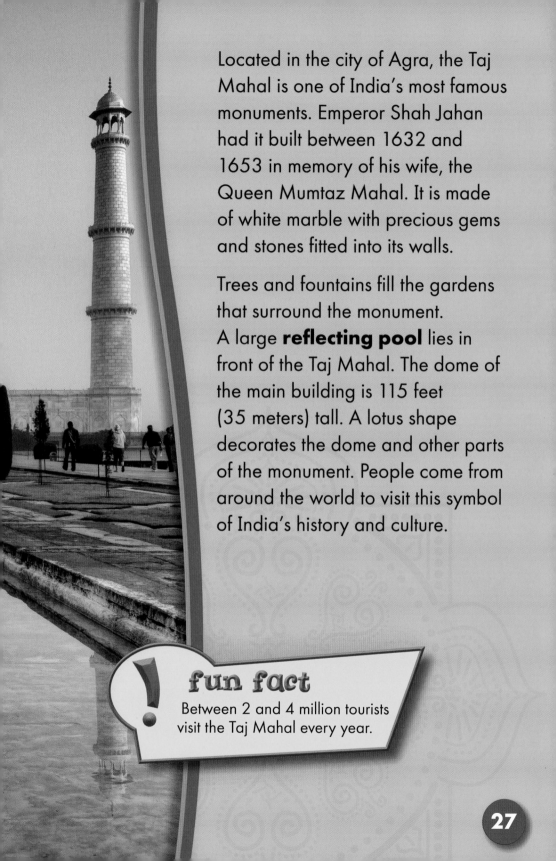

Located in the city of Agra, the Taj Mahal is one of India's most famous monuments. Emperor Shah Jahan had it built between 1632 and 1653 in memory of his wife, the Queen Mumtaz Mahal. It is made of white marble with precious gems and stones fitted into its walls.

Trees and fountains fill the gardens that surround the monument. A large **reflecting pool** lies in front of the Taj Mahal. The dome of the main building is 115 feet (35 meters) tall. A lotus shape decorates the dome and other parts of the monument. People come from around the world to visit this symbol of India's history and culture.

fun fact

Between 2 and 4 million tourists visit the Taj Mahal every year.

Fast Facts About India

India's Flag

India's flag has three horizontal stripes of saffron, white, and green. Saffron stands for piety and patriotism, white stands for purity and peace, and green stands for prosperity. A wheel in the middle of the flag stands for progress. It has 24 spokes to symbolize the hours in a day. The flag was adopted on July 2, 1947.

Official Name: Republic of India

Area: 1,269,219 square miles (3,287,263 square kilometers); India is the 7th largest country in the world.

Capital City:	New Delhi
Important Cities:	Mumbai, Kolkata, Bangalore
Population:	1,173,108,018 (July 2010)
Official Language:	Hindi
National Holiday:	Independence Day (August 15)
Religions:	Hindu (80.5%), Muslim (13.4%), Other (6.1%)
Major Industries:	farming, manufacturing, mining, services
Natural Resources:	oil, natural gas, iron ore, diamonds, coal, bauxite, fish, farmland, wood
Manufactured Products:	clothing, chemicals, steel, cement, machinery, software, medicine, transportation equipment
Farm Products:	rice, wheat, tea, cotton, sugarcane
Unit of Money:	rupee; the rupee is divided into 100 paise.

Glossary

chutney—a blend of sugar, vinegar, spices, and fruits; chutney is used to top many foods in India.

constitution—the basic principles and laws of a nation

cricket—a game played with a ball, bats, and low stands called wickets

diet—the food and drink normally consumed by a person

fast—to choose not to eat

gulf—part of an ocean or sea that extends into land

information technology—the technology of developing and maintaining computer systems and software

mangrove forests—thick areas of trees and shrubs along coastlines

native—originally from a place

natural resources—materials in the earth that are taken out and used to make products or fuel

non-violent protest—using peaceful means to try to change things

peninsula—a section of land that extends out from a larger piece of land and is almost completely surrounded by water

plateau—an area of flat, raised land

Ramadan—the ninth month of the Islamic calendar; Ramadan is a time when Muslims fast from sunrise to sunset.

reflecting pool—a large, shallow pool that reflects something of importance

summit—the highest point of something

tandoori ovens—large clay ovens heated with a charcoal or wood fire

textiles—fabrics or clothes that have been woven or knitted

tributaries—streams or rivers that flow into a larger stream or river

tuition—the cost of going to school and getting an education

United Kingdom (U.K.)—a state that includes England, Scotland, Wales, and Northern Ireland

To Learn More

AT THE LIBRARY

Apte, Sunita. *India*. New York, N.Y.: Children's Press, 2009.

Kalman, Bobbie. *India the Culture*. New York, N.Y.: Crabtree Publishing, 2010.

Swan, Erin Pembrey. *India*. New York, N.Y.: Children's Press, 2002.

ON THE WEB

Learning more about India is as easy as 1, 2, 3.

1. Go to www.factsurfer.com.

2. Enter "India" into the search box.

3. Click the "Surf" button and you will see a list of related Web sites.

With factsurfer.com, finding more information is just a click away.

Index

The images in this book are reproduced through the courtesy of: Tian Zhan, front cover, pp. 26-27;
Maisei Raman, front cover (flag), p. 28; Juan Eppardo, pp. 4-5; Dinodia Dinodia/Photolibrary, pp. 6-7;
Juan Martinez, pp. 7 (small top), 8-9, 9 (small), 11 (middle & bottom), 15, 18; Ben Pipe/The Travel
Library/Photolibrary, p. 7 (small bottom); Carlos Caetano, pp. 10-11; Niels Holm, p. 11 (top); Paul
Prescott, pp. 12-13, 19 (right); Dinodia Images/Alamy, p. 14; Amit Somvanshi/Photolibrary, p. 16;
David Pearson/Alamy, p. 17; Dana Ward, p. 19 (left); Asia Images Group Pte Ltd/Alamy, p. 20 (small);
DreamPictures/Getty Images, pp. 20-21; Louise Batalla Duran/Alamy, p. 22; Eva Gruendemann, p. 23
(top); Joe Gough, p. 23 (bottom); Idris Ahmed/Alamy, p. 24; Kharidehal Abhirama Ashwin, p. 25; Ajay
Bhaskar, p. 29 (bill & coin).